# Discipled

# Discipled

## What the *Holy Bible* Says about Being a CHRISTIAN

Priscilla Doremus

Copyright © 2017 Priscilla Doremus. All rights reserved.

A Seven Bears Publishing production

ISBN:

978-1-7344259-5-6 (papeback)

978-1-7344259-6-3 (hardback)

978-1-7344259-7-0 (epub)

Unless otherwise indicated, all Scripture quotations are taken from the Holy Bible, New Living Translation, copyright © 1996, 2004, 2007, 2013, 2015 by Tyndale House Foundation. Used by permission of Tyndale House Publishers, Inc., Carol Stream, Illinois 60188.

All rights reserved.

# Dedication

This book is dedicated to you, the reader.
May you know what it means
to be a Christian.

# Contents

| | | |
|---|---|---|
| | Author's Note | 1 |
| | Prologue | 3 |
| One | What Is A Christian? | 5 |
| Two | Counting The Cost | 17 |
| Three | Living The Christian Life | 23 |
| Four | The Tempter's Snare | 41 |
| Five | Intimacy With God | 51 |
| Six | Finishing Strong | 59 |
| Seven | Stories Of Courage And Encouragement | 71 |
| Eight | The Journey | 91 |
| | About the Author | 93 |
| | Helpful Resources | 95 |

# Author's Note

THIS BOOK IS WRITTEN BASED ON THE BELIEF THAT THE *Holy Bible* is more than a history book. It is the divinely-inspired, inherent Word of God—the *One True and Living God*.

In no way does this author pretend to have the market cornered on divine wisdom, nor do I assert myself as authority, scholar, or anything more than a follower of Christ, longing to share the indescribable joy that I have found in knowing Him in a real and personal way. I do not have all of the answers. But, I know the One who does.

You should know that I am praying for you as you read this book, that you would see beyond its imperfections to find and know the boundless love of Jesus Christ for yourself, and that you would study His Word, the *Holy Bible*, in its entirety.

May the Holy Spirit guide you, and may our Heavenly Father bless you beyond anything you could ever ask or imagine every day for the rest of your life as you seek to know Him more.

# Prologue

YOU CALL YOURSELF A CHRISTIAN, BUT DO YOU REALLY know what it means to be a Christian?

Is a Christian someone who has been raised in the church or in a Christian family? Perhaps you believe a Christian to be someone whose good deeds outweigh the bad. Or, maybe you know that a Christian is a follower of Jesus Christ, but aren't really sure what that means, exactly.

A Christian *is* a follower of Christ, but do you know who Christ is? Do you know what He expects of you?

Many people I encounter who call themselves Christians—and some who are serving in leadership positions in churches today—have no idea what it truly means to be a Christian. I believe with all my heart that becoming a Christian is the most important decision you and I will ever make.

Perhaps you have recently decided to follow Jesus. Maybe you are not sure if you are a Christian or not. Or, possibly you've been a Christian for many years. Wherever you find yourself, my prayer for you is that you will know fully what it means to have a real, personal relationship with Jesus Christ.

In the following pages, together with the *Holy Bible* and the Holy Spirit as your guide, may you learn what it *really* means to call yourself a *Christian*.

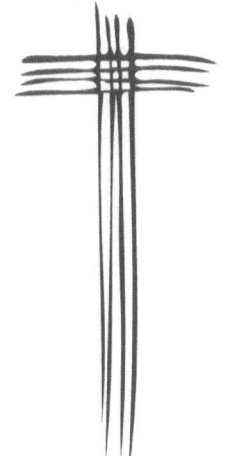

# What is a Christian?

*Jesus called out to them, "Come, follow me, and I will show you how to fish for people!"*

—*Matthew 4:19*

CHRISTIANS ARE FOLLOWERS OF JESUS CHRIST. SO, WHAT does it really mean to be His *follower*? A *follower* is defined as one who adheres to the teachings of, and models the behavior of another; an apprentice; a disciple. So, a Christian is someone who adheres to the teachings of, and models the behavior of Jesus. It's really that simple.

Sadly, what we see demonstrated in the lives of many who call themselves Christian sits in stark contrast to the radical life of Jesus we find evidenced in Scripture. The *Holy Bible* reminds us to prove by the way we live that we have repented of our sin and turned to God (Matthew 3:8).

So, what does it really look like to *follow* Jesus? That is often the complex part.

What does He require of me? How can I be sure I'm living the right way, doing the right things, the things He wants me to do? How do I know whether or not I'm going to heaven?

These are all very important questions.

But, before we know what a Christian is, we must first have a good understanding of who Jesus Christ really is. The best place to find the answer to that question and all of these questions is in the *Holy Bible*.

## Who Is Jesus?

In the *Holy Bible*, we learn that Jesus is the Son of God. Luke 1:35, tells us the account of God sending the angel, Gabriel, to visit Mary. The Scripture tells us, "The angel replied, 'The Holy Spirit will come upon you, and the power of the Most High will overshadow you. So the baby to be born will be holy, and he will be called the Son of God.'" The Christian believes that Jesus is man, conceived by the Holy Spirit.

The *Holy Bible* also calls Jesus the Son of Man. Mark 10:45 says, "For even the Son of Man came not to be served but to serve others and to give his life as a ransom for many."

Jesus is the Messiah promised to the nation of Israel in the Old Testament to be their deliverer. The word *Messiah* comes from the Hebrew word *mashach* or *mashiach* which means anointed. In Scripture, those who were anointed were set apart, consecrated by God for a holy purpose.

In Luke 5:32, Jesus tells us the purpose for which He has come,

"I have come to call not those who think they are righteous, but those who know they are sinners and need to repent." In Luke 12:49-50, Jesus tells us further, "I have come to set the world on fire, and I wish it were already burning! I have a terrible baptism of suffering ahead of me, and I am under a heavy burden until it is accomplished." Jesus carried a heavy burden so that we wouldn't have to.

And, Jesus is one with God the Father. John 10:30 tells us, "The Father and I are one."

The answer to the question, "Who is Jesus?" is far greater than words could ever say, or I could ever express in these pages.

He is rich in mercy (Ephesians 2:4). He is just and perfect (Deuteronomy 32:4). He is tender and compassionate to those who fear Him. He is like a father to His children (Psalm 103:13). He gives and forgives generously (2 Corinthians 9:8; Isaiah 55:7). Every good gift we have, and every perfect gift we have is from Him (James 1:17). He is the cornerstone (Psalm 118:22). He is the author and finisher of our faith (Hebrews 12:2). He is the giver of life (Psalm 36:9). He is the friend of tax collectors and sinners (Matthew 11:19). He is the light of the world (John 8:12). He is jealous for us (Exodus 34:14). Jesus is Wonderful Counselor, Mighty God, Everlasting Father, Prince of Peace (Isaiah 9:6). He is perfect (1 John 1:5). He is love defined (1 John 4:8), and He is so, so much more to each one of us, personally.

The person of Jesus Christ, though he lived over two thousand years ago, dwells among us—He is all around us—today. Those who believe in Him recognize Him and see His miracles for their spiritual eyes are open to His work in the world all around them.

Do you want to know Him, *really* know Him? Then, you must seek Him with all your heart. He is nearer than you think. Acts 17:27 tells us, "His purpose was for the nations to seek after God and perhaps feel their way toward him and find him—though he is not far from any one of us."

## How Did Jesus Live?

Jesus lived a life of love, a life of service, a life of sacrifice. He celebrated with people, He cried with them, He healed them, He forgave them, He served them, He taught them.

And, in many ways, He lived a life much like you and me. There was work to be done, Jewish classes to attend, family gatherings and parties of all sorts. His daily life didn't really diverge drastically from the norm until the beginning of His ministry at about age thirty (Luke 3:23), and since He was thirty-three years old at the time of His death, Jesus did quite a bit of living, loving, giving, teaching, forgiving, sacrificing and serving in that brief three-to-four-year span of time.

Jesus never lived exclusively unto Himself. He loved being with people–the people He came to save. His mission was to find sinners and lead them to repentance, to seek and save the lost (Luke 5:32; 19:10). But, He also loved spending time with the Father, and often withdrew from the crowds and went into the wilderness to pray (Luke 5:16).

He lived passionately and compassionately, caring deeply for the needs of others. Jesus once passed the funeral procession of a young man, a widow mother's only son. He was so moved with compassion for the young man's mother that Jesus raised him from the dead (Luke 7:11-15).

Jesus served others. From turning water into wine and healing the lame and blind to washing the disciples' feet and feeding crowds of people in miraculous ways, Jesus was a servant to all. Though He spoke with authority and confidence, Jesus was never prideful or arrogant. He was meek; God's power restrained.

He lived sacrificially, demonstrating His great love for us. Jesus laid down His perfect sinless life for you and for me that we might have the opportunity to receive eternal life.

Jesus was a miracle worker.

The perfect, sinless life and brief ministry of Jesus set the world on fire, and that fire is still burning in the lives of His followers all over the world today.

## Why Did Jesus Have to Die?

Jesus' death, burial, and resurrection was as necessary as the perfect, sinless life that He lived before the watching world.

In Matthew 17:21, Jesus begins to tell His disciples that it is necessary for Him to suffer many terrible things, to be killed, but that on the third day He would rise from the dead. The disciples had a difficult time understanding why this would happen or why it would be necessary. Peter, in particular, even reprimanded Jesus when he heard this.

Yet, Hebrews Chapter Nine and Chapter Ten explain why Christ's death was the perfect and necessary sacrifice. His death fulfilled the new covenant between God and all mankind. No longer do we need to feel guilty day after day for the sins we have committed, as under the old covenant. Jesus' death ushered in a new way. The God of the Old Testament seems different than the God of the New Testament not because He is, but because there is a new covenant—one that requires our complete faith and trust in Him, and our obedience. A covenant with laws written in our minds and on our hearts. The fulfillment of this covenant manifests itself in magnificent, immeasurable real fruit on a daily basis.

Thanks be to God and His Son, Jesus the Christ, for this remarkable and immaculate sacrifice!

## What Did Jesus Teach?

Jesus taught people how to love and how to live. He met people at their point of need, and with unspoiled discernment, assessed the condition of each and every heart before speaking or taking action.

He was an amazing story-teller, and often shared His lessons in the form of parables. Some parables were simple to understand, and some had hidden or veiled meanings.

He taught all people about a new commandment, not an addendum to the ten they already knew, but rather the completion of the ten they already knew. In John 13:34, Jesus said, "So now I am giving you a new commandment: Love each other. Just as I have loved you, you should love each other."

It sounded simple enough. But, Jesus' way of loving was radically different and distinct from anything those around Him had ever experienced before. It is distinct from any human love we know, as well. Yet, Jesus makes a way for us to understand this love through the Holy Spirit. Romans 5:5 tells us that He has given us the Holy Spirit to fill our hearts with His love.

To recount all of the things that Jesus taught would be to regurgitate the Scripture in its entirety, and so very much more. Not even Scripture can contain all that Jesus taught and did before His resurrection.

## How Does One Become a Christian?

Romans 10:9-10 tells us, "If you openly declare that Jesus is Lord and believe in your heart that God raised him from the dead, you will be saved. For it is by believing in your heart that you are made right with God, and it is by openly declaring your faith that you are saved."

There is a story in the *Holy Bible* about a man named Nicodemus (John 2:23-3:21) who came to speak with Jesus at night. It was clear to Nicodemus that Jesus had been sent by God, but the concept of being *born again* was puzzling to him. Jesus explained that we must be born of water—the physical birth, and that we must also be born of the Spirit if we want to see the Kingdom of God. But, Nicodemus didn't understand what it actually meant to be born of the Spirit. What does that look like?

Jesus explained that being born of the Spirit is something that cannot be explained in human terms, but that by faith we simply believe.

Think about a young child before they have been tainted, corrupted by the world. They trust. They believe! God wants us to believe in Him the same way.

Matthew 18:3 tells us, "Then he said, 'I tell you the truth, unless you turn from your sins and become like little children, you will never get into the Kingdom of Heaven.'" It is this simple, child-like faith we must possess in order to please God.

The experience of how someone becomes a Christian varies widely between individuals, but according to Scripture, every salvation experience includes the following parts, though you may know them by different names:

1. Believe – We must believe that Jesus Christ is God's son, that He lived a perfect, sinless life, that He died on the cross for our sins, and was resurrected from the dead (Romans 10:9-10).

2. Receive – We receive His gift of salvation (Romans 4:16).

3. Repent – We must repent of our sin and turn to God (Luke 13:3, 5). Repentance is leaving our old, sinful life behind and turning to follow Christ.

4. Share – We must openly declare our faith in Jesus Christ with others (Mark 8:38; Romans 10:9-10). We can't hide Him or be ashamed of Him.

Baptism occurs after salvation as a demonstration to the watching world that we have repented of our sin and turned to God. It neither determines nor precludes our salvation, but is an act of obedience to God.

In the *Holy Bible*, the act of baptism was first introduced by John the Baptist who came preparing the way for Jesus Christ. The word *baptism* or *baptize* is the transliteration of the Greek word *baptizo*, meaning "to immerse."

Jesus was baptized by John the Baptist which brought great pleasure to the Father. Matthew 3:16-17 recounts, "As soon as Jesus was baptized, he went up out of the water. At that moment heaven was opened, and he saw the Spirit of God descending like a dove and alighting on him. And a voice from heaven said, 'This is my Son, whom I love; with him I am well pleased'" (NIV).

But, why must I do all of these things when some passages of Scripture tell me I need only to believe (Acts 16:31; Ephesians 2:8)? It is simply because true believing is active, and all of these things are evidence of this act of believing.

When we begin a personal relationship with Jesus, a change takes place. We are forgiven and free. God gives us a new heart of flesh to replace our stony, stubborn heart, and a transformation begins to take place within us. The *Holy Bible* tells us in Second Corinthians 5:17 that when we become a follower of Jesus, we become a new person. Our old life is gone, and a new life has begun!

How beautiful to have a new life, regardless of our age or any past sin we have ever committed. We are forgiven and free!

## Can I Renounce My Christianity?

The *Holy Bible* tells us in Isaiah 43:13, "From eternity to eternity I am God. No one can snatch anyone out of my hand. No one can undo what I have done." It also tells us in in Romans 8:38, "And I am convinced that nothing can ever separate us from God's love. Neither death nor life, neither angels nor demons, neither our fears for today nor our worries about tomorrow—not even the powers of hell can separate us from God's love."

These verses of Scripture clearly depict God's love and protection of us and for us as His followers, but there is more to the story. Our God is the very definition of love, yes. And, He is also just. When a person stops believing, they are choosing to reject God.

Scripture tells us in Romans 11:22, "Notice how God is both kind and severe. He is severe toward those who disobeyed, but kind to you if you continue to trust in his kindness. But if you stop trusting, you also will be cut off." You should read the entire Book of Romans, as it has much to say about the life lived as a Christian.

The *Holy Bible* goes on to give us a warning like no other with regard to renouncing our faith in Jesus Christ in Hebrews 6:4-6 when it says, "For it is impossible to bring back to repentance those who were once enlightened—those who have experienced the good things of heaven and shared in the Holy Spirit, who have tasted the goodness of the word of God and the power of the age to come—and who then turn away from God. It is impossible to bring such people back to repentance; by rejecting the Son of God, they themselves are nailing him to the cross once again and holding him up to public shame."

How tragic the very thought, the consideration of casting God's perfect love aside.

## The Parable of the Farmer Scattering Seed

Being a Christian doesn't end with the decision to follow Jesus. That decision is just the beginning. Jesus tells a parable in Matthew 13:1-23 explaining what happens to various people who hear His Word.

In the story, a farmer scatters seed, and there are four different things that happen to the seeds. Some of the seeds fall along a walkway and the birds eat them. These seeds represent people who hear the Word of God, but don't understand it. The devil snatches the Word of God planted in their hearts before it has a chance to take root and grow. Other seeds fall on rocky soil. They sprout quickly, but soon wilt in the hot sun since they don't have deep roots. These seeds represent the people who receive the gospel message with joy, but when trouble comes, they quickly fall away because they are not rooted deeply in Christ. A third group of seeds fell among thorns that grew up and choked the plants. They represent those who hear God's message, but the cares of life and the lure of wealth crowd their life so that no fruit is produced. Finally, the fourth group of seeds falls on good soil which represents those who hear and truly understand God's Word. Their lives produce an amazing harvest of good fruit for God's Kingdom.

We have the freedom to choose which seeds we will become.

Which will you be?

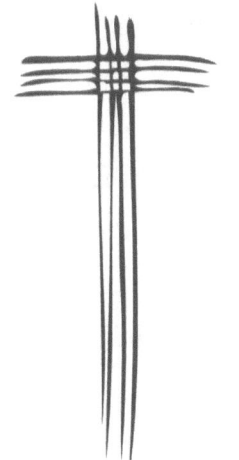
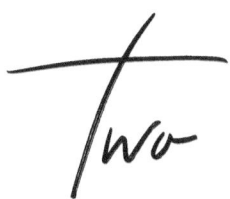

## Counting the Cost

*"But don't begin until you count the cost. For who would begin construction of a building without first calculating the cost to see if there is enough money to finish it?"*

—*Luke 14:28*

THERE IS A COST INVOLVED IN FOLLOWING CHRIST. MAKE no mistake about it. The cost? You must trade in *your* way for His.

The Christian life requires us to give up our own plans and dreams for God's. The plans God has for us are far better and different than plans we make for ourselves. He weaves together every strand, every fiber of our lives with the lives of others until it becomes a tapestry so brilliant that we cannot even begin to imagine it. His desire is that all would come to know Him, to believe in Him, to find *real* life in Him.

Jim Elliot, a missionary who was martyred while attempting to share Jesus with the Huaorani people in Ecuador is credited with saying, "He is no fool who gives what he cannot keep to gain that which he cannot lose." It is picture of our life with Jesus Christ.

C. S. Lewis says it like this, "Aim at Heaven and you will get earth 'thrown in': aim at earth and you will get neither."

And, the *Holy Bible* says it this way, "If you cling to your life, you will lose it; but if you give up your life for me, you will find it" (Matthew 10:39).

When we choose to do things our way and live life on our own terms, following our own selfish desires, we come to the end of our earthly life empty, and with far worse eternal consequences. The benefits we receive for following Jesus are far greater than any cost of giving up our own way.

## How May My Relationships Change?

When we become a follower of Jesus, our relationships change, too. Not everyone will be excited about the change in us, the transformation of our heart and life.

In John 15:18-19, Jesus tells us, "If the world hates you, remember that it hated me first. The world would love you as one of its own if you belonged to it, but you are no longer part of the world. I chose you to come out of the world, so it hates you."

Becoming a Christian is a very sobering way to discover which side your friends and family are really on. As you discover more about the character of Jesus and what He expects of you through reading the *Holy Bible*, you will discover how radical His teaching really is. His love is fundamentally different from what the world teaches. His light within you will be a magnet—like a moth to a flame—for those who are searching, and it will be repulsive to those who reject Him.

Not everyone who *claims* to be a follower of Christ is willing to follow what His Word teaches. There are many who pick and choose what they believe in Scripture, ignoring the things which they simply do not want to practice. The *Holy Bible* has a great deal to say about such individuals. As a new believer or old, it is important to choose a strong inner circle of believers who practice the teachings of Christ with all of their heart, all of their being.

## How Can Salvation Be Free and Costly at the Same Time?

Perhaps you've heard this before:

"This is not what I signed up for! I know God loves me, and He would definitely *not* want me to put up with, or be treated *like this!*"

It is a common misconception, this notion of earthly life somehow being easier or better for Christians than for non-Christians. Being treated *like this* is exactly what you signed up for when you decided to follow Jesus.

In Matthew Chapter Ten, Jesus prepares the twelve apostles before sending them out into the world. In Matthew 10:22, He says to them, "And all nations will hate you because you are my followers. But everyone who endures to the end will be saved."

It is the same with Christians in non-Christian nations today. Jesus calls us to a life that is different. Those who do not know God cannot understand the life of faith. Christianity is radically different, and the *Holy Bible* is the most radical book you will ever read.

There is arguably no greater cost in becoming a Christian than the change in our relationships with others. Luke 14:26-27 tells us, "If you want to be my disciple, you must, by comparison, hate everyone else—your father and mother, wife and children, brothers and sisters—yes, even your own life. Otherwise, you cannot be my disciple. And if you do not carry your own cross and follow me, you cannot be my disciple."

This Scripture is telling us that Jesus is to have first place in our lives. Obedience to Him is to be our number one priority.

Second Corinthians 6:14 says, "Don't team up with those who are unbelievers. How can righteousness be a partner with wickedness? How can light live with darkness?"

In this passage, Paul is issuing a call for us to form our tightest bonds and closest relationships with other Christians. An inner circle of faith is necessary not only for fellowship and encouragement, but for spiritual growth, as well. Attempting to maintain close bonds with non-believers is more than counterproductive. It simply will not work. We cannot live life as both a Christian and a non-Christian.

When we share Christ with those close to us and they fail to accept Him by faith, our relationships change, and it can be very difficult. Christians are often treated very badly by those who do not understand the life of faith.

Yet, in spite of how the world treats Christians, it is the Christian's love for others and service to them that defines the Christian life. Jesus tells us in John 13:35, "Your love for one another will prove to the world that you are my disciples."

The Christian life is not something to be entered into lightly. Jesus cautioned us with regard to this in Luke Chapter Nine. There was a man who claimed that he wanted to follow Jesus, but first wanted to return home and say goodbye to his family. In Luke 9:62 we read, "But Jesus told him, 'Anyone who puts a hand to the plow and then looks back is not fit for the Kingdom of God.'" Perhaps Jesus knew that the man's family would urge him to stay, leading him away from Jesus' call upon his life—His perfect plan and purpose.

Many people suppose that they can call themselves Christians, yet still live in the worldly manner to which they have grown accustomed. They continue living in sin, unrepentant, and yet you see them in church services each and every Sunday morning.

God's Word tells us plainly how we should deal with such individuals in First Corinthians 5:11, which says, "I meant that you are not to associate with anyone who claims to be a believer yet indulges in sexual sin, or is greedy, or worships idols, or is abusive, or is a drunkard, or cheats people. Don't even eat with such people."

Paul is speaking specifically about those in the church who claim to be Christians in this passage of Scripture, rather than non-Christians. He wants us to demonstrate a very clear picture to the watching world that Christians are different.

As Christians, we are called to read the Scripture, to study the Scripture, and to share God with others at every opportunity, as we are admonished to always be ready to explain our hope as a believer to anyone who asks (1 Peter 3:15).

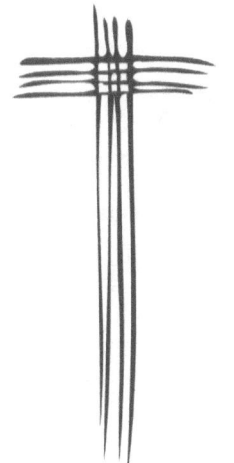

## Living the Christian Life

*But if we are living in the light, as God is in the light,*
*then we have fellowship with each other,*
*and the blood of Jesus, his Son, cleanses us from all sin.*

—*1 John 1:7*

AFTER THE DECISION TO FOLLOW JESUS CHRIST COMES THE activity of living out that decision each and every day. If we claim to be a Christian, our life is no longer our own. We belong to God. Our desires become one with His desires.

First John 3:10 tells us, "So now we can tell who are children of God and who are children of the devil. Anyone who does not live righteously and does not love other believers does not belong to God."

Being a real follower of Christ means something. It means saying "no" to the world's way, and saying "yes" to God. We must be obedient to His Word, the *Holy Bible*.

In Luke 9:23, Jesus puts it this way, "Then he said to the crowd, 'If any of you wants to be my follower, you must turn from your selfish ways, take up your cross daily, and follow me.'"

That means that each and every morning when you get up, you must make a conscious choice to follow God, to do things His way, rather than your own way. There is no such thing as a part-time Christian. Walking in obedience to Jesus Christ is a conscious, daily choice. The world should see a very distinct difference in the way a Christian lives, each and every day.

The *Holy Bible* also tells us what that distinct difference looks like. Galatians 5:22-23 tells us, "But the Holy Spirit produces this kind of fruit in our lives: love, joy, peace, patience, kindness, goodness, faithfulness, gentleness, and self-control. There is no law against these things!" The Christian life exhibits this fruit to the world around them on a regular basis.

The *Holy Bible* reinforces this by telling us that a Christian is to prove their Christianity by the way they live. Luke 3:8 tells us to "Prove by the way you live that you have repented of your sins and turned to God. Don't just say to each other, 'We're safe, for we are descendants of Abraham.' That means nothing, for I tell you, God can create children of Abraham from these very stones."

I encourage you to read Second Peter 1:3-11. This passage of Scripture reminds us that God has given the Christian many precious promises to ensure our successful growth and development. If we follow God's plan, we will never fall away from Him (Second Peter 1:10).

But, living the Christian life can sometimes become confusing when we take our eyes off of God and listen to others—even for a moment.

There are some bearing the name, *Christian*, who live their lives trying to obey every letter of the law in their own strength. When they fail in this effort, they beat themselves up in frustration, and promise God that they'll do better.

Still others live their lives doing whatever they please whenever they please, having no concern for obeying Christ, and simply whitewash their every sin by the blood of Jesus Christ and by His grace.

My friend, neither of these approaches will please God.

God desires that we allow His Holy Spirit to guide us each and every day. He wants our obedience, but not simply for the sake of obedience. It is a daily choice, a moment-by-moment choice, to give up our own selfish way and follow the Holy Spirit's way. And yes, when we fall, the blood of Jesus, His mercy and grace, cleanse us from all unrighteousness. But our intent should always be to obey Him, to live pleasing to Him.

Read Galatians Chapter Five.

Becoming a slave to the things of God is true freedom. Let me say that another way. When we choose to allow the Holy Spirit to control us rather than sin, we are truly free! Sin is a deadly taskmaster, but God isn't. His way is life. His way is love! Remember God's wisdom is foolishness to the masses. The yoke God gives us is easy and His burden is light (Matthew 11:30). When we try to live life our way, it is actually much more burdensome than choosing God's way.

## What Does Following Christ Look Like on a Daily Basis?

*Joyful are those who listen to me, watching for me daily at my gates, waiting for me outside my home!—Proverbs 8:34*

Being a Christian is an active pursuit. There is nothing passive about it. It begs that we are about spreading the good news of God everywhere we go, in everything we say and do. It requires us to give up our own selfish ways and desires and obey Christ Jesus in service to others. Yet, it is not burdensome.

Following is one small example of what the Christian life looks like to me. It looks like James.

James gets up early each morning, reads his *Holy Bible*, prays, exercises, bathes, and eats a light breakfast. He goes to work as a substitute teacher in a high school for special needs children where he joyfully serves and inspires everyone around him. While there, he goes the extra mile in every way—even picking up trash as he walks through the building. When he finishes there, he conducts a worship service at a prison twenty miles away.

One day a week, James conducts a church service at a local nursing home and visits people in his church. He is always busy helping others and giving to those in need. He never worries about money. God has always met his every need, and he gives generously. In the evening after dinner, he writes the things that God has laid upon his heart for future generations to read. He reads the *Holy Bible* again, spends time in prayer, and goes to bed.

James is an eighty-four-year-old widower who loves God. I can see this love oozing out of every pore in his being. He is joyful, vigorous, and he inspires me.

There are many examples of the Christian life. James is a brilliant man who could have been a doctor, a lawyer, or any number of things of his own choosing, but God called him to be a pastor at a young age. James honored that call, retiring at age eighty-two due to pancreatic cancer. After a successful surgery and a period of recovery, this is the example I find: a courageous Christian who has never given up, never stopped serving, and who daily takes up his cross to follow Christ in service to others.

He could have easily sat back and given up, taking the world's tack that he's paid his dues and done his time. But, James listens to the voice of God and heeds His call—every day.

Are you listening to the Spirit's voice telling you what following Him looks like for *you* today?

He may call you to be a doctor or a ditch digger. He may call you to a noble profession or an ordinary one, for He is the potter and we are the clay. Whatever His call, your life lived in accordance with His plan will produce a blessing for many generations to come.

## Some Things We Shouldn't See in a Christian's Life

### *The Differences*

Remember again that the *Holy Bible* tells us to prove by the way we live that we are followers of Christ (Matthew 3:8; Luke 3:8). One of the ways that Christians do that is through their speech. A Christian's speech is not the same as everyone else's speech. It is a reflection of the change that has occurred on the inside. Ephesians 4:29 tells us, "Don't use foul or abusive language. Let everything you say be good and helpful, so that your words will be an encouragement to those who hear them."

Proverbs 15:28 says, "The heart *of the godly thinks carefully before* speaking; the mouth *of the wicked overflows with evil words."* And, Luke 6:45 reiterates, *"A good man out of the good treasure of his heart brings forth good; and an evil man out of the evil treasure of his heart brings forth evil. For out of the abundance of the heart his mouth speaks."*

Another distinct difference in the Christian's life is the manner in which they love. Theirs is a giving love, a serving love, a sacrificial love. It is distinct from the world's definition of love.

Christians are not miserly, either. The *Holy Bible* says, "The wicked borrow and never repay, but the godly are generous givers" (Psalm 37:21).

Christians are also not self-centered. Philippians 2:3 tells us, "Don't be selfish; don't try to impress others. Be humble, thinking of others as better *than yourselves."*

God, in His great kindness, even tells us the behaviors that he hates.

"There are six things the Lord hates—no, seven things he detests: haughty eyes, a lying tongue, hands that kill the innocent, a heart that plots evil, feet that race to do wrong, a false witness who pours out lies, a person who sows discord in a family" (Proverbs 6:16-19).

May we pray earnestly for God to guard and protect us from the temptation to practice these sins.

## Examples of the Christian Walk

It is helpful to have an example, someone to emulate, in our pursuit of knowing Christ. A couple of caveats before we begin: (1) There is no greater example than Jesus, Himself; and (2) imperfect people should never be placed on pedestals, and that is not the intent here. The intent is to give us a picture of how the heart committed to Christ changes the life's response to all things. The *Holy Bible* gives us many examples of the Christian walk—both good and bad.

Daniel was a good example of what it means to be a Christian. Though he lived before the birth of Christ, his life exemplified the heart change that Jesus died for. The *Holy Bible* tells us that Daniel was honorable and trustworthy in all of his dealings—so much so that he outshined all of the other administrators in the kingdom of Babylon. These administrators were jealous of Daniel because they knew the king planned to make him the head of the entire empire. Scripture tells us in Daniel 6:4, "Then the other administrators and high officers began searching for some fault in the way Daniel was handling government affairs, but they couldn't find anything to criticize or condemn. He was faithful, always responsible, and completely trustworthy." That is what a Christian looks like.

Noah was a good example of what it means to be a Christian, too. Read Genesis 6:9-22. Here, we find a person who longed to please God and walk in obedience to all that He commanded.

Job was also an excellent example of what following God is all about. In Job 1:1, we read that Job was a man of complete integrity, a blameless man. You can read his entire story in the Book of Job.

We talk a bit more about Daniel, Noah, and Job in Chapter Seven.

The *Holy Bible* is full of many other accounts of those who followed God faithfully, like Abraham, Moses, Elijah, Joseph, Enoch, David, Paul, John, Peter, James, Timothy and many more. We also find those who turned away from Him, like Cain and Judas. Each of these men had a choice, whether to be a slave to sin which leads to death, or a slave to obedience, that leads to righteousness (Romans 6:15-18). Each of us has that same choice today.

## Tools of the Trade

As with any grand pursuit, there are tools and best practices that enable you to live the Christian life successfully. Those tools include: study of the *Holy Bible*, prayer, and fellowship with other believers. Each one plays an important part in our development, growth, and maturity as a Christian.

## Bible Study

Reading your *Holy Bible* each and every day is essential—not only for us to learn who the triune God is—but, Scripture reading also has a way of setting us in the proper frame of mind as we start and end each day. I recommend that you read in the morning and in the evening, as you start and end each day. This will help frame your day, your thoughts, and begin to teach you what God expects from you each and every day in living the Christian life. Through this time, God will begin to mold and shape your life into the image of Christ, His Son.

## Prayer

We could write endlessly about prayer. Ask a Christian that you respect about the power and personal impact of prayer in his or her life. It is an amazing gift to the believer.

The *Holy Bible* tells us that we should, "Never stop praying" (I Thessalonians 5:17). Prayer is a powerful tool. It is communication with God, and Scripture is filled with many examples of how we should pray, as well as how we shouldn't pray. One of the most notable passages of Scripture in which Jesus teaches us how to pray is Matthew 6:9-13. Christians refer to this as the Lord's Prayer.

The *Holy Bible* teaches us to be persistent (Ephesians 6:18) and thankful (1 Timothy 2:1) in our prayers, and it teaches us that the condition of our heart has a direct impact on the effectiveness of our prayer life. I can't imagine life without prayer, our direct communication with the one true and living God.

David said in Psalm 116:2, "Because he bends down to listen, I will pray as long as I have breath!" Imagine it, the Creator of the Universe bends down to listen when you pray. How could we not take advantage of this overwhelming gift?

## *Inner Circle of Believers*

Christians need each other. One of the many astounding and beautiful aspects of living the Christian life is that we are not expected to go it alone. The *Holy Bible* admonishes us in Hebrews 10:25 when it says, "And let us not neglect our meeting together, as some people do, but encourage one another, especially now that the day of his return is drawing near."

Jesus, Himself, prayed for the unity of all believers everywhere in John Chapter Seventeen. It is a beautiful prayer, revealing the heart of our precious Savior that you should take the time to read.

We also receive help and encouragement from our Christian brothers and sisters. As Galatians 6:2 tells us, "Share each other's burdens, and in this way obey the law of Christ."

The road of life is filled with many obstacles and temptations, and we can become discouraged or disheartened at times along the way. Having a fellow believer with more experience to encourage, pray, and offer wise counsel cannot be underestimated as we navigate life's journey. And, as we begin to grow in our faith, it is important for us to come alongside fellow believers who are just beginning their journey in the Christian life. They need the same encouragement, prayer, and wise counsel we received at critical times in our life.

Matthew 18:20 comforts us with these words, "For where two or three gather together *as my followers, I am there among them.*"

## Staying the Course

*You were running the race so well. Who has held you back from following the truth?—Galatians 5:7*

You've accepted Jesus Christ as your personal Savior, your guide, your daily companion and Lord of your life. So, how do you stay on track and avoid the pitfalls and temptations that kept you from Him in the past? How do you keep from falling back into bad patterns of behavior?

Proverbs 3:6 holds the key, "Seek his will in all you do, and he will show you which path to take." We must have a heart that desires to please God, and we must make choices that are pleasing to Him. Living the Christian life requires discipline, as Psalm 119:9 reminds us, "How can a young person stay pure? By obeying your word."

If we want to stay on track in our Christian walk, then we will need to obey God, and in order to do that, we need to know what He requires of us. There are no shortcuts.

Scripture tells us about the pitfalls and temptations we will face. And, it tells us how to avoid them and stay the course. It also gives us words of comfort if or when we go astray. The book of Psalms is full of wisdom about staying on the right path.

Psalm 25:8 tells us, "The Lord is good and does what is right; he shows the proper path to those who go astray."

Psalm 119:35 says, "Make me walk along the path of your commands, for that is where my happiness is found."

And, Psalm 32:8 promises us, "The Lord *says,* 'I will guide you along the best pathway for your life. I will advise you and watch over you.'"

We stay the course one right decision at a time, one choice to resist temptation at a time, one act of obedience to Christ's voice at a time.

## O, How He Loves You and Me

*And I am convinced that nothing can ever separate us from God's love. Neither death nor life, neither angels nor demons, neither our fears for today nor our worries about tomorrow—not even the powers of hell can separate us from God's love.—Romans 8:38*

In the fifteenth Chapter of Luke, Jesus tells three different parables, painting a vivid picture of just how much He loves us—each and every one of us that He has made.

The Parable of the Lost Sheep in Luke 15:3-7 reads, "So Jesus told them this story: 'If a man has a hundred sheep and one of them gets lost, what will he do? Won't he leave the ninety-nine others in the wilderness and go to search for the one that is lost until he finds it? And when he has found it, he will joyfully carry it home on his shoulders. When he arrives, he will call together his friends and neighbors, saying, 'Rejoice with me because I have found my lost sheep.' In the same way, there is more joy in heaven over one lost sinner who repents and returns to God than over ninety-nine others who are righteous and haven't strayed away!"

In the Parable of the Lost Coin (Luke 15:8-10), a woman loses one of ten silver coins. She sweeps her entire house and searches carefully to find it. When she finds it, she calls all her friends and neighbors together to rejoice with her in finding it. Verse ten tells us, "In the same way, there is joy in the presence of God's angels when even one sinner repents."

The Parable of the Lost Son (Prodigal Son) is probably the most well-known story. It is the story of a son who asks for an early inheritance from his father. This *entitled* son soon wastes all of his father's inheritance in wild living and finds himself starving. He begs a job from a pig farmer and soon realizes the error of his ways, longing to return home to his father in humbled repentance. When the father sees his son returning home in the distance, he runs to meet him, having his servants bring the finest robe, a ring for his finger, and sandals for his feet. It is cause for great celebration!

That is how it is in heaven when just one sinner repents! Our Heavenly Father adores us so much that if you had been the only lost sheep, He still would have sent His one and only son to die on the cross, just for you.

Oh, how He loves you and me.

## Spotting a True Christian

How can you spot a true Christian?

There is an important caution here. The *Holy Bible* tells us that God alone knows every human heart (2 Chronicles 6:30). Scripture goes on to tell us that we do not even know all the sins lurking in our own hearts (Psalm 19:12).

While we cannot judge another man's heart, the *Holy Bible* does give us ways to judge another person's motives by examining the way that they live.

1. Fruit – Jesus uses fruit in a number of ways to help us understand what the Christian life looks like when it is lived out on a daily basis. The *Holy Bible* uses the analogy of trees and the kind and amount of fruit they produce to teach us this important truth (Matthew 7:15-20; Matthew 12:33; Luke 6:44). Jesus tells us the fruits that are evident in a Christian's life are: love, joy, peace, patience, kindness, goodness, faithfulness, gentleness and self-control (Galatians 5:22-23).

2. Faith – A Christian has faith. Hebrews 11:6 tells us, "And it is impossible to please God without faith. Anyone who wants to come to him must believe that God exists and that he rewards those who sincerely seek him." A Christian believes. Scripture refers to Christians as *believers* for this reason.

3. Obedience – A Christian is obedient to God's commands, and

he or she also teaches others to do likewise. Matthew 28:20 confirms this when it says, "Teach these new disciples to obey all the commands I have given you. And be sure of this: I am with you always, even to the end of the age."

4. Habits – Christians practice habits and have behaviors that are pleasing to God. There are many of these, and we must read Scripture to know what they are. We talk about four of these habits in the next section, but there are many more.

# Four Important Habits of a Christian

We talked about *Tools of the Trade* for successful Christian living, and there is some overlap between these important tools and good Christian habits.

In order to live a victorious Christian life, it is vital to spend time reading God's Word, the *Holy Bible*, every day. God communicates with us and teaches us through His Word. Though we may not always understand everything we read in the *Holy Bible* each day, we do grow closer to Christ the more we read His Word. Just as you grow closer to people and understand them better the more time you spend with them, so we grow closer to God and begin to understand Him better as we spend more time with Him, by reading His Word.

Another important aspect of getting to know God is by spending time with Him in prayer. Prayer is a two-way conversation with our loving Heavenly Father that comes directly from our heart. Jesus taught us how to pray by providing us with many examples in

His Word: Matthew 6:5-15; Luke 1:1-13; Luke 5:16; Luke 18:1-8; John 17, and many others.

The Holy Bible tells us in 1 Thessalonians 5:17 to, "Never stop praying." Part of our prayer time should always be listening for the gentle whisper of God speaking to us in return. Trying to grow as a Christian without daily prayer and Bible reading is like depriving a seed of water and sunlight—neither has a good result.

A third important habit in living a victorious Christian life is sharing Him with others each and every day. How do we do this? It is an overflow of the Spirit of God within us as Christians, and we simply can't stop it when we are walking with Him. It manifests itself as simply as a smile from the heart, and meets each and every person at their point of need.

Matthew 28:19-20, referred to as the Great Commission, commands us, "Therefore, go and make disciples of all the nations, baptizing them in the name of the Father and the Son and the Holy Spirit. Teach these new disciples to obey all the commands I have given you. And be sure of this: I am with you always, even to the end of the age."

When we have a relationship with Jesus, it is selfish for us to keep Him to ourselves and not share Him with others. Often Christians are hesitant to share Christ with others for fear they do not have all of the answers, but we can and should always share what He has done and is doing in our own lives. Personal stories are meaningful, relatable, and helpful to others. When we share God's Word and our personal stories, the *Holy Bible* tells us it makes a difference. Isaiah 55:11 confirms this by telling us, "It is the same with my word. I send it out, and it always produces fruit. It will accomplish all I want it to, and it will prosper everywhere I send it."

A fourth habit that is important in the Christian life is that of giving. Scripture discusses many ways that believers should give. The tithe in Scripture was the giving of the first and best ten percent of the believer's increase to the work of the church. The word *tithe* means tenth. It is the one area of the Christian life in which we are invited to test God.

Malachi 3:10 tells us, "Bring all the tithes into the storehouse so there will be enough food in my Temple. If you do," says the Lord of Heaven's Armies, "I will open the windows of heaven for you. I will pour out a blessing so great you won't have enough room to take it in! Try it! Put me to the test!"

I have found this to be true. We can never *outgive* God. When we give God our first and best, He will even rebuke the devourer on our behalf (Malachi 3:11).

We find the principle of giving throughout Scripture, and we learn that the godly are generous givers to those in need. Nothing we use on this earth is our own. It all belongs to God, and we are to be good stewards of all that He has entrusted to us.

## Becoming a Servant

*"But among you it will be different. Those who are the greatest among you should take the lowest rank, and the leader should be like a servant."*
*—Luke 22:26*

The Son of Man came not to be served but to serve (Matthew 20:28; Mark 10:45). He washed the disciples feet as an act of service, humility, and cleansing. If Jesus came to serve others, then how much more are we to serve those in need around us?

This idea of service and humility is infused throughout Scripture. When we serve others, we teach them the ways of Jesus. In First Peter Chapter Five, we find Peter instructing elders and young men regarding this subject, as well.

First Peter 5:2 says, "Care for the flock that God has entrusted to you. Watch over it willingly, not grudgingly—not for what you will get out of it, but because you are eager to serve God."

Philippians 2:3 tells us, "Don't be selfish; don't try to impress others. Be humble, thinking of others as better than yourselves."

And, Micah 6:8 encourages us with these words, reminding us that a life lived in service to God is not filled with overwhelming requirements, "No, O people, the Lord *has told you* what is good, and this is what he requires of you: to do what is right, to love mercy, and to walk humbly with your God."

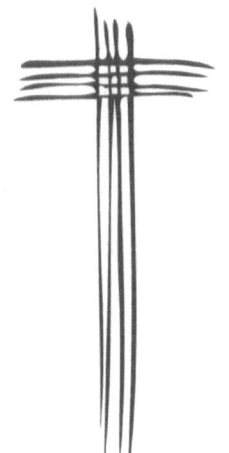

## *four*

# The Tempter's Snare

*Stay alert! Watch out for your great enemy, the devil.*
*He prowls around like a roaring lion,*
*looking for someone to devour.*

—*1 Peter 5:8*

AN IMPORTANT PART OF LIVING THE CHRISTIAN LIFE IS knowing that there is an enemy. That enemy is Satan. To deny his existence is to give him the victory from the start.

But, who is Satan? And, how does he operate? We can find the answers in the *Holy Bible*.

There are many names for Satan in the *Holy Bible*. He is called Lucifer, Evil One, Prince of this World, Dragon, Beelzebub, the King of Babylon, and the Greek and Hebrew names Apollyon and Abaddon which transliterate to the English word, "destroyer," among others.

Truly, Satan is the destroyer. The *Holy Bible* tells us in John 10:10 he is a thief who "comes to steal, kill, and destroy."

Satan doesn't act alone, either. He has a band of demons to assist him in carrying out his evil plans. And, since we are at war with him constantly, it is important to know the way our enemy operates.

## The Enemy's *Modus Operandi*

When facing any adversary, it is best to know their *modus operandi* in order to defeat them. The *Holy Bible* tells us how to recognize our adversary, the devil, and it also tells us how to overcome him through the power of the Holy Spirit working in and through our lives.

We have clues into Satan's *modus operandi* simply in the names and nicknames given to him. He is the Accuser in Job 2:1. He is the prince of demons in Matthew 12:24. He is a dangerous trap in Matthew 16:23. He is the ruler of this world in John 12:31. He is the god of this world in Second Corinthians 4:4. Revelation 12:9 calls Satan the great dragon, ancient serpent, and the one deceiving the whole world.

He is a deceiver. In Genesis 3:13 we read about his deception of Eve in the Garden of Eden.

He is a liar. One of the chief ways in which Satan operates is by taking a small piece of truth and packaging it in a great big lie. This is another way in which he deceives us. We are hooked by the shred of truth, and often fail to recognize the much bigger lie surrounding it.

John 8:44 says he was "a murderer from the beginning and a hater of truth." This passage also tells us he is the "father of liars".

Satan can disguise himself as an angel of light. In Second Corinthians 11:14, Paul is talking about false Christians working out devilish deeds in the church when he says, "But I am not surprised! Even Satan disguises himself as an angel of light."

Satan and his followers produce bad fruit (Matthew 12:33). Their works result in bad outcomes—not good. However, the world has become so twisted that we often fail to recognize this bad fruit for what it is. At first glance, these actions appear to be good, but dig a little deeper. When we are viewing the world through the eyes of the Holy Spirit, it is plain to see.

The love of God is not in him. First John 3:10 instructs us, "So now we can tell who are children of God and who are children of the devil. Anyone who does not live righteously and does not love other believers does not belong to God."

Knowing these things, we must line up every teaching, every doctrine, and every decision with the Word of God, the *Holy Bible*, so as not to be led astray by the many wolves in sheep's clothing that we encounter in the world.

## What Does the Holy Bible Say About Temptation?

The *Holy Bible* has a great deal to say about temptation.

First, it tells us what causes temptation. In James 1:14-15, the *Holy Bible* tells us, "Temptation comes from our own desires, which entice us and drag us away. These desires give birth to sinful actions. And when sin is allowed to grow, it gives birth to death." Remember that God does not tempt us (James 1:13).

Next, it tells us that all temptations can be overcome. First

Corinthians 10:13 says, "The temptations in your life are no different from what others experience. And God is faithful. He will not allow the temptation to be more than you can stand. When you are tempted, he will show you a way out so that you can endure."

Jesus understands what we're going through when we're tempted. He was tempted in all ways just as we are, yet He did not sin (Hebrews 2:18; 4:15; Matthew 4:1-11). Jesus encourages us to keep watch and pray so that we won't give in to temptation (Mark 14:38), adding that the spirit is willing, but the body is weak.

We need fellow Christians to come alongside us to strengthen us in the battle against sin. Galatians 6:1 says, "Dear brothers and sisters, if another believer is overcome by some sin, you who are godly should gently and humbly help that person back onto the right path. And be careful not to fall into the same temptation yourself."

The *Holy Bible* also issues a stern warning against our leading others into temptation in Luke 17:1, when it says, "One day Jesus said to his disciples, "There will always be temptations to sin, but what sorrow awaits the person who does the tempting!"

When our heart pines for the things of this world more than the things of God, then we are easily led astray and yield to temptation, becoming entrenched and entangled in sin.

## How Do We Fight the Enemy and Say "No" to Temptation?

God wants us to be victorious over sin, and so He tells us in His Word how to say "no" to sin. First Corinthians 15:57 tells us, "But thank God! He gives us victory *over* sin *and death through our Lord Jesus Christ."*

In the story of Cain and Abel in the book of Genesis, Cain becomes angry when his sacrifice is rejected by God. But, Cain's sacrifice was not given from a heart that longed to please God.

In Genesis 4:7, God spoke to Cain about the situation. He said, "You will be accepted if you do what is right. But if you refuse to do what is right, then watch out! Sin is crouching at the door, eager to control you. But you must subdue it and be its master."

So, how do we subdue sin and become its master?

Ephesians 6:10-18 tells us how to do this, reminding us that we are not fighting flesh and blood enemies, but the spiritual forces of evil in the heavenly realms. It is by putting on the whole armor of God: the belt of truth, the breastplate of righteousness, shoes of peace, the shield of faith, the helmet of salvation, and the sword of the Spirit, which is God's Word. This is how we subdue sin and become its master.

Scripture goes on to encourage us in James 4:7 when it says, "So humble yourselves before God. Resist the devil, and he will flee from you."

## The Role Intellect Plays in Temptation

Do you consider yourself too smart or too intellectual for Christianity?

It is healthy to learn and to educate ourselves about faith. But, we must always ask ourselves, has our scholarly debate become the means by which we rationalize our blatant disobedience of God's commands? Are we using our intellect to justify our own sin?

The *Holy Bible* tells us in 1 Corinthians 10:12, "If you think you are standing strong, be careful not to fall."

Scripture warns us about falling for every new idea that comes along, too. We must grow and become mature in our relationship with Christ so that we know what we believe and do not fall victim to false teaching.

Ephesians 4:14 refers to this maturity when it says, "Then we will no longer be immature like children. We won't be tossed and blown about by every wind of new teaching. We will not be influenced when people try to trick us with lies so clever they sound like the truth."

Our intellect will never be more powerful than when we have faith in the one true and living God.

## The New Age

*Now I will tell you new things, secrets you have not yet heard.*
*—Isaiah 48:6b*

The New Age Movement that has gained popularity in the United States in recent decades espouses two very frightening lies: (1) There are many ways to God; and, (2) Truth and power are within us all.

These ideas are clearly from Satan, and seek to pull us away from the truth of God. They are ideas that are crafted using something we discussed earlier, Satan's favorite *modus operandi*: Take a small truth and wrap it in a great big lie.

The *Holy Bible* tells us clearly that there is but one way to God. Matthew 7:3 says, "You can enter God's Kingdom only through the narrow gate. The highway to hell is broad, and its gate is wide for the many who choose that way."

John 17:3 explains, "And this is the way to have eternal life—to know you, the only true God, and Jesus Christ, the one you sent to earth."

Truth and power are found in God alone. We can know His truth, and His Holy Spirit living inside us can embody His truth, but the truth is *His*.

John 14:6 says, "Jesus told him, 'I am the way, the truth, and the life. No one can come to the Father except through me.'"

If we will fill our hearts and minds with God's truth, His Spirit will flow freely from every pore in our being. That is the truth of every age, and this truth never changes.

## Biblical Examples

### *Cain*

When it comes to temptation, I am often drawn to the story of Cain and Abel in the Fourth Chapter of Genesis, which was briefly mentioned earlier. In the story, Cain became a farmer and Abel was a shepherd. At harvest time, Cain brought some of his crops to the Lord as a sacrifice, and Abel brought the best portions of the firstborn lambs from his flock. God accepted Abel's offering, but rejected Cain's gift, which made Cain very angry.

God, being the loving Father of all life, counseled Cain regarding the situation. Listen to what the Scripture says in Genesis 4:6-7, "'Why are you so angry?' the Lord asked Cain. 'Why do you look so dejected? You will be accepted if you do what is right. But if you refuse to do what is right, then watch out! Sin is crouching at the door, eager to control you. But you must subdue it and be its master.'"

Unfortunately, Cain did not heed the instruction of his loving Heavenly Father, and suffered the consequences. He became a homeless wanderer.

## Joseph

A very different example of temptation response is found in the Thirty-Ninth Chapter of the Book of Genesis, the story of Joseph. Joseph had been sold into slavery by his jealous brothers, and purchased as a slave by Potiphar, Captain of the Guard for Pharaoh, King of Egypt.

Joseph was faithful to Potiphar in everything that he did, and God blessed Potiphar's household because of Joseph. Potiphar placed Joseph in charge of all his household affairs, having complete trust in him.

Potiphar's wife, however, had plans of her own for Joseph. She longed to have an affair with him, but Joseph refused. One day, when they were alone in the house, Potiphar's wife was so aggressive toward Joseph that in order to avoid her, he had to run from the house, leaving his cloak behind in her hands. She lied to Potiphar, telling him that Joseph tried to seduce her, but when she screamed, Joseph ran, leaving his cloak behind.

As a result, Joseph spent a long time in prison for a crime he did not commit. But, God was faithful. Joseph's obedience and waiting was not in vain, and it did not go unnoticed. After God interpreted the Pharaoh's dream through Joseph, Pharaoh made Joseph second in command of all Egypt. You can read more about Joseph's story starting in Genesis Chapter Thirty-seven.

There are rewards for not yielding to temptation, though we must often exercise patience, allowing that patience to have its perfect work in our lives (James 1:4).

God gives the same instruction and counsel to you and to me today that He gave to Cain so long ago. And, which way will you choose? Will you choose to go your own way in sin, and suffer as Cain did? Or, will you choose God's way, the way of life, as Joseph did?

James 1:12 promises us, "God blesses those who patiently endure testing and temptation. Afterward they will receive the crown of life that God has promised to those who love him."

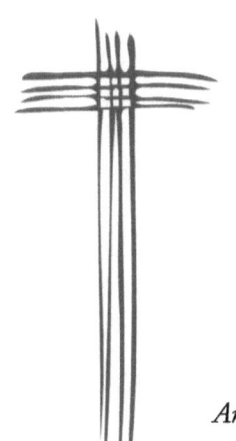

# five

## Intimacy with God

*And Solomon, my son, learn to know the God of your ancestors intimately. Worship and serve him with your whole heart and a willing mind. For the L*ORD *sees every heart and knows every plan and thought. If you seek him, you will find him. But if you forsake him, he will reject you forever.*

—*1 Chronicles 28:9*

THERE ARE TWO PEOPLE MENTIONED IN THE *HOLY BIBLE* who had such intimacy with God that they did not die. Those two people were Enoch and Elijah.

In Genesis Chapter Five, we learn that Enoch was sixty-five years old when he fathered Methuselah, who lived longer than any other person on record at nine hundred sixty-nine. Enoch was also the great-grandfather of Noah. This passage of Scripture tells us that after Methuselah was born, Enoch walked in close fellowship with God for three hundred more years, having other sons and daughters. And then one day, Enoch disappeared because God took him (Genesis 5:24).

In the case of Elijah, recounted in Second Kings Chapter Two, we read that Elijah and Elisha were walking and talking when a chariot of fire appeared. Verse eleven says, "As they were walking along and talking, suddenly a chariot of fire appeared, drawn by horses of fire. It drove between the two men, separating them, and Elijah was carried by a whirlwind into heaven."

Hebrews 11:5 tells us that Enoch was taken because of his faith, and because he was known to live a life that was pleasing to God.

I can imagine no greater intimacy than to walk in harmony with God, our Father, to walk in purity, having close fellowship with Him. Being intimate with God, being made right with Him, is only accomplished by faith in Him (Romans 3:30; Galatians 2:16; Philippians 3:9).

## How Do I Draw Close to God?

*Come close to God, and God will come close to you. Wash your hands, you sinners; purify your hearts, for your loyalty is divided between God and the world.—James 4:8*

In principle, drawing close to God is very clear, as outlined in the verse above. So, why do we encounter difficulty in following through?

The *Holy Bible* gives us the answer.

First, a lack of faith can keep us from drawing close to God. As mentioned before, Hebrews 11:6 tells us, "And it is impossible to please *God* without faith. Anyone who wants to come to him must believe that God exists and that he rewards those who sincerely seek him." If we do not have faith, we are not living a life that is pleasing to God, and we cannot be close to Him.

Second, sin separates us from God. When we harbor sin in our heart, cling to pet sins, and refuse to repent of strongholds of sin in our life, we distance ourselves from God. In Isaiah 59:2 we read, "It's your sins that have cut you off from God. Because of your sins, he has turned away and will not listen anymore."

Satan uses every manipulation and distraction imaginable to steal our focus from God and limit our effectiveness once we've accepted Christ as our Savior. So, we must focus our pursuit of Christ on a daily basis. Christianity is not an effortless endeavor.

But, the Holy Spirit helps us in this endeavor. As Romans 8:26 offers these words of comfort and encouragement, "And the Holy Spirit helps us in our weakness. For example, we don't know what God wants us to pray for. But the Holy Spirit *prays for us with groanings that cannot be expressed in words."*

Our single-minded love and faith in Jesus Christ will draw us closer still to God.

## The Importance of Purity

*We prove ourselves by our purity, our understanding, our patience, our kindness, by the Holy Spirit within us, and by our sincere love.*
*—2 Corinthians 6:6*

You cannot pump your life full of garbage and expect good things to come out of it. Let me say that again: *You cannot pump your life full of garbage and expect a good result.*

More specifically, you cannot watch movies filled with profanity and violence and expect to draw closer to God. You cannot listen to music with negative or provocative lyrics and expect your life to be pure and unscathed by it. You cannot play violent video games or spend your time with those who do, and not become desensitized. These things change you—not for the better—and, they allow Satan a wide-open door into every area of your life.

There is a children's song that talks about things so important in the life of every Christian, regardless of age, and it goes like this:

> *Oh, be careful little eyes,*
> *what you see*
> *Oh, be careful little eyes,*
> *what you see*
>
> *For the Father up above,*
> *is looking down in love,*
> *So be careful little eyes*
> *what you see.*

This song goes on to talk about what we hear, do, say, and where we go. It is a reminder of the importance of keeping our lives pure. We are reminded ninety-one times to be careful in the New Living Translation of the *Holy Bible*.

The world's impure distractions and constant lures of entertainment are the thorns, the cares of the world, that choke us, preventing us from producing good works and receiving the fullness of God's blessing in our lives as recounted in the *Parable of the Farmer Scattering Seed* discussed in Chapter One.

## How Does Obedience Help Me Stay Close to God?

*Obey my commands and live! Guard my instructions as you guard your own eyes.—Proverbs 7:2*

Our sin separates us from God (Isaiah 59:2). Obedience to God is how we prove our love for Him and our faith in Him. It allows us to live in fellowship with Him (1 John 3:24). Consider the relationship between a good father and his child. When the child acts in obedience, it is pleasing to the father. There is nothing that the father would not do for this obedient child, as the bond is strengthened between the two in this way, causing the relationship to grow.

It is even greater for us in relationship to our Heavenly Father because His love for us is so much greater than any earthly love. Our obedience is pleasing to Him, and this good Father would move heaven and earth for us.

Our obedience to God also keeps us on the path that He has designed for our life. When we are obedient to Him, we hear His voice telling us which way we should go (Isaiah 30:21).

The *Holy Bible* tells us that if we obey God's laws and teach others to do likewise, we will be called greatest in the Kingdom of Heaven (Matthew 5:19). The converse is true, as well.

Obedience to God's laws also fills us with joy, which fills us with gratitude, enhancing our longing to please God. Proverbs 29:18 says, "When people do not accept divine guidance, they run wild. But whoever obeys the law is joyful."

We must also remember that when it comes to obedience, partial obedience is disobedience. We must obey the commands of God fully to be pleasing to Him, which is a reflection of our heart's condition.

Consider the Old Testament story of King Saul in First Samuel Chapter Fifteen. In the story, God commanded King Saul to "completely destroy the entire Amalekite nation—men, women, children, babies, cattle, sheep, goats, camels, and donkeys." Instead, King Saul brought back King Agag, and kept the best of everything else. It was clear disobedience. Yet, when Samuel confronted King Saul with his sin, Saul said, "I *did* obey."

Do you ever do that?

Disobedience can be very costly, not just in the here and now, but for generations to come. In King Saul's case, it cost him the crown, and nearly wiped out the entire Jewish race.

Conversely, the rewards for obedience to God are unending and reach far beyond our wildest imagination.

## Does My Walk With God Remain Constant?

*And as we live in God, our love grows more perfect. So we will not be afraid on the day of judgment, but we can face him with confidence because we live like Jesus here in this world.—1 John 4:17*

Our walk with God is not constant. It is in constant change. We are either moving toward God or away from Him at any given time throughout our earthly life.

There is a constant spiritual tug-of-war going on, and that which we choose to feed on a daily basis is that which will win out—whether spirit or flesh. Though Satan cannot steal our salvation once we have accepted Jesus Christ as Savior, if we choose to feed our flesh rather than the spirit, Satan will steal our effectiveness and God's best plan for our life.

When we allow God to change us, Second Corinthians 3:18 tells us, "So all of us who have had that veil removed can see and reflect the glory of the Lord. And the Lord—who is the Spirit—makes us more and more like him as we are changed into his glorious image."

Our daily choices must reflect a longing to obey our Heavenly Father in order for us to continue to be transformed into His image, His likeness. There are no shortcuts. There is no easy way out. Good habits and self-discipline are required. These things are a constant choice, and there is effort required on our part.

Though we change, and our relationship to Him changes, there is great comfort in knowing that our Savior never changes. He remains the same (James 1:17).

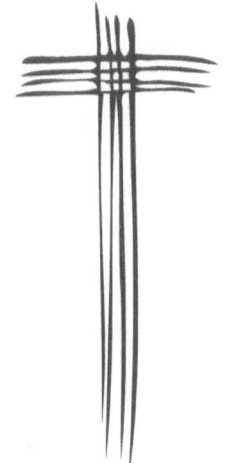

# six

## Finishing Strong

*I have fought the good fight, I have finished the race,
and I have remained faithful.*

—2 Timothy 4:7

BECOMING A CHAMPION IN ANY FIELD REQUIRES TRAINING. It requires practice. Training and practice, in order to be most effective, demand that we be focused on the goal. When we are focused on a goal, we are able to visualize our success. We picture ourselves achieving the goal.

Becoming a champion in the Christian life and living victoriously as we follow Jesus embodies this same principle.

Hebrews 12:1-2 puts it this way, "Therefore, since we are surrounded by such a huge crowd of witnesses to the life of faith, let us strip off every weight that slows us down, especially the sin that so easily trips us up. And let us run with endurance the race God has set before us. We do this by keeping our eyes on Jesus, the champion who initiates and perfects our faith. Because of the joy awaiting him, he endured the cross, disregarding its shame. Now he is seated in the place of honor beside God's throne."

What is it that is slowing you down? Is there a stronghold of sin in your life that requires repentance? Have you stopped focusing your eyes on the true champion, Jesus Christ? Or, are you still trying to live a double life?

It is impossible to have a victorious Christian life while continuing to do things the world's way. The *Holy Bible* reminds us in Matthew 6:24 that we cannot serve two masters. This particular passage of Scripture is talking about God and money as the two masters. We could just as easily say that we cannot serve God and the world. They are opposing forces.

As Christians, God has called us to a transformed mind, a new way of thinking.

## How Will God Enable You to Live a Victorious Life?

*But you belong to God, my dear children. You have already won a victory over those people, because the Spirit who lives in you is greater than the spirit who lives in the world.—1 John 4:4*

God wants you and me to live a victorious life. He is never pleased or happy to see us struggle and fall.

Isaiah 41:10 tells us, "Don't be afraid, for I am with you. Don't be discouraged, for I am your God. I will strengthen you and help you. I will hold you up with my victorious right hand."

It is the Holy Spirit's power at work within us that enables us to live a victorious life. Yet, many fail to recognize or fully realize this power in their lives. It is often due to a lack of faith.

Scripture tells us in First John 5:4, "For every child of God defeats this evil world, and we achieve this victory through our faith." We need only live in the power and the reality of this truth. But, how do we do this? It sounds so simple. Why is it such a struggle?

Our faith grows as our relationship with Christ grows. As Colossians 2:7 tells us, "Let your roots grow *down into him, and let your lives be built on him. Then your* faith *will* grow *strong in the truth you were taught, and you will overflow with thankfulness.*"

## Where Does the Victory Come From?

*I wait quietly before God, for my victory comes from him.—Psalms 62:1*

Scripture tells us clearly that the victories we experience in life come from God our Father. But, is there anything we can do to make experiencing this victory any more likely to occur?

Taking up our cross daily, choosing by an act of our will to follow Christ each and every day of our lives is a victorious choice. It is a choice to allow the Holy Spirit to control our life this day, to love, to live by faith, to walk in obedience to God, and to not allow the world to corrupt us.

When we do these things, we receive our victory from God, and a peace that passes all understanding (Philippians 4:7).

Psalm 62:7 says, "My victory *and honor* come *from God alone. He is my refuge, a rock where no enemy can reach me.*"

And, Isaiah 12:2 tells us, "See, God has come *to save me. I will trust in him and not be afraid. The Lord God is my strength and my song; he has given me* victory."

Praise be to God, the source of all our victory!

## What Does Victorious Living Produce in My Life?

*But the Holy Spirit produces this kind of fruit in our lives: love, joy, peace, patience, kindness, goodness, faithfulness, gentleness, and self-control. There is no law against these things!—Galatians 5:22-23*

When we are living as Christ desires, the Holy Spirit is evident in our lives. The fruit of the Holy Spirit is evident as we go about our everyday activities, regardless of what those activities happen to be. The character of Jesus exudes through every pore of our being as our human fabric is interwoven with His.

Victorious living also draws others to Jesus Christ like a moth to a flame. Others desire the same life and want to know what it is that makes the Christian different. This difference is in the very definition and in the person of Jesus Christ as we allow Him room to live in us, transforming us into a new creation. "For in him we live and move and exist. As some of your own poets have said, 'We are his offspring'" (Acts 17:28).

Our righteous living turns others from a life of sin, too (Malachi 2:6).

The *Holy Bible* tells us that godly, righteous living has many other blessings that accompany it. The godly will live in the presence of God

(Psalm 140:13). They will have everything they need (Matthew 6:33). They will be at rest and live in safety (Isaiah 32:18). Those who take delight in the Lord will receive the desires of their heart (Psalm 37:4).

These are but a few of the promises God gives to us.

# A Word About Discipline

*Train up a child in the way he should go, and when he is old he will not depart from it.*—Proverbs 22:6

Discipline is an important aspect of living the Christian life successfully. There are two types of discipline: the world's way and God's way.

The world's discipline can be cruel and damaging. It is viewed as punishment. It teaches hatred and resentment. God's way of discipline is loving and kind. It instructs, and it develops wisdom and sound character.

Neither type of discipline is pleasant at the time it is experienced; and, this is where the similarities end.

To demonstrate the difference, a teenage boy was driving to piano lessons for the first time. He had been given directions, and had been told the way, as well. On his first day, the boy got lost and missed the entire lesson which could not be refunded.

The worldly father in anger demanded that the boy get back into the car and drive to piano lessons to show he knew the way and would not miss the lesson again. He gave the boy no instruction and was silent the entire time.

The father seeking to do things God's way required that the boy get back into the car and drive to piano lessons, also. But, he instructed the boy the entire way, telling him the things he had done right, advising of landmarks, road signs, and how to avoid getting lost in the future. He instructed on things unrelated to the route, as well, because he loved the child.

The *Holy Bible* tells us in Hebrews 12:10-11, "For our earthly fathers disciplined us for a few years, doing the best they knew how. But God's discipline is always good for us, so that we might share in his holiness. No discipline is enjoyable while it is happening—it's painful! But afterward there will be a peaceful harvest of right living for those who are trained in this way."

Two types of discipline, yet a fool despises them both and plunges headlong into destruction, while a wise man can learn from either form of discipline.

## Two Biblical Champions

### Elijah

*Elijah was as human as we are, and yet when he prayed earnestly that no rain would fall, none fell for three and a half years!—James 5:17*

Elijah was such a mighty man of faith that he did not taste of death, as mentioned previously. You should read his entire story in First and Second Kings.

Scripture also gives us a wonderfully encouraging story about

Elijah, his humanness, and how God enables us to be overcomers in each and every situation we face.

In First Kings Chapter Eighteen, we read how Elijah, by the power of God, had just won quite a contest to prove to King Ahab and all the people of Israel who the One True and Living God was. This contest ended in the killing of all the prophets of Baal. When the evil Queen Jezebel heard what had happened, she promised to have Elijah killed before twenty-four hours had passed.

Elijah was afraid for his life, and ran all day into the wilderness, sat down under a solitary broom tree, and prayed that he might die. He was so very discouraged that this is what he prayed, "I have had enough, Lord," he said. "Take my life, for I am no better than my ancestors who have already died" (1 Kings 19:4b).

Elijah fell asleep under that broom tree, and God sent an angel to bring him freshly baked bread, water and to give him more rest for the long journey ahead. What a miracle! He endured with God's help to become a champion of faith.

The same encouragement and provision God gave to Elijah, He gives to you and me, as well.

## John the Baptist

*I tell you the truth, of all who have ever lived, none is greater than John the Baptist. Yet even the least person in the Kingdom of Heaven is greater than he is!—Matthew 11:11*

John the Baptist came to the Judean wilderness with a very simple message: "Repent of your sins and turn to God, for the Kingdom of Heaven is near" (Matthew 3:2). He came to prepare the way for Jesus.

John told of the coming of Jesus, as prophesied in the Old Testament. The two were family. John the son of Elizabeth, and Jesus the son of Mary, her cousin. The two men were just about six months apart in age.

John went from place to place along both sides of the Jordan River preaching that people should be baptized. Why? Their baptism was an outward sign that they had repented of their sin and turned to God.

This man wasn't afraid to speak the truth, or to confront even the king in his sin. He baptized Jesus, and truly prepared the way for Him to minister to the masses of people who needed to find their way to God's truth—from that day forward.

John was a humble man, and though his obedience to Christ eventually lead to him being martyred (Mark 6:14-29), he accomplished the purpose and finished well the race God had set before him. John the Baptist was a true champion.

Does this mean that you must be martyred to be great in God's Kingdom? No, but it does mean you must be willing to go wherever God leads you and do whatever He asks.

## The Ultimate Reward

*Anyone with ears to hear must listen to the Spirit and understand what he is saying to the churches. To everyone who is victorious I will give fruit from the tree of life in the paradise of God.—Revelation 2:7*

The rewards for living a victorious life, a life that has remained faithful to Christ until the end, are limitless.

The Book of Revelation is filled with examples of these rewards God has prepared for those who are faithful to Him. In Revelation 15:2, John paints a beautiful picture of a heavenly scene involving those who have been victorious. The passage reads, "I saw before me what seemed to be a glass sea mixed with fire. And on it stood all the people who had been victorious over the beast and his statue and the number representing his name. They were all holding harps that God had given them."

Scripture goes on to tell us more about the victorious and their rewards. They will not be harmed by the second death, the eternal, spiritual separation from God in the fiery lake of burning sulfur (Revelation 2:11; Revelation 21:8).

The victorious will receive some of the manna that has been hidden away in heaven, and they will receive a new name that only they and God will understand. This name will be engraved on a white stone (Revelation 2:17). Imagine it. Your own new name, ascribed to you by God, Himself.

Those who obey Christ to the very end will receive authority over all the nations (Revelation 2:26).

Revelation 3:5 promises, "All who are victorious will be clothed in white. I will never erase their names from the Book of Life, but I will announce before my Father and his angels that they are mine."

Revelation 3:12 tells us, "All who are victorious will become pillars in the Temple of my God, and they will never have to leave it. And

I will write on them the name of my God, and they will be citizens in the city of my God—the new Jerusalem that comes down from heaven from my God. And I will also write on them my new name."

Revelation 3:21 says, "Those who are victorious will sit with me on my throne, just as I was victorious and sat with my Father on his throne." Best of all, Revelation 21:7 promises us, "All who are victorious will inherit all these blessings, and I will be their God, and they will be my children." My friend, there is no better place on earth than the road that leads to heaven.

## Too Late

*When the master of the house has locked the door, it will be too late. You will stand outside knocking and pleading, "Lord, open the door for us!" But he will reply, "I don't know you or where you come from."*
—*Luke 13:25*

I would be remiss to finish on such a high note without at least mentioning the warning that one day we will run out of time on this earth. There are a number of popular Christian songs out today containing the line "it's never too late." And, while I know the writers have the best of intentions and mean nothing but encouragement, the words are not true.

The *Holy Bible* teaches us that one day it will be too late for us to turn to Christ. One day it will be too late for us to choose to be obedient to Him. And, one day the door to the Master's house will be closed and locked.

So often, we want to paint our picture with a broad brush that accepts everyone into God's Kingdom because God is love (1 John 4:8). But, the road that leads to Him is a narrow road, and only a few ever find it (Matthew 7:14). It is the road of obedience, of faith, and there is no substitute for that faith-filled obedience. We cannot choose our own way and God's way, too.

Satan would have you to believe that a loving God would not make you give up your own way and your own desires, but that is a lie. It is the love of God that requires you to give up your own way—your way of selfishness and sin. And, what God promises you in return is far, far greater than anything or anyone you will ever give up.

"Look! I stand at the door and knock. If you hear my voice and open the door, I will come in, and we will share a meal together as friends" (Revelation 3:20).

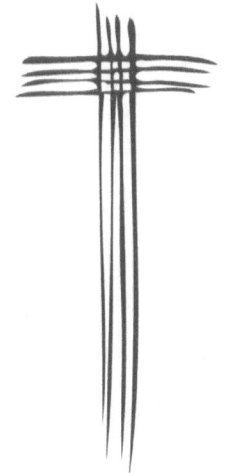

# seven

## Stories of Courage and Encouragement

*So we have been greatly encouraged in the midst of our troubles and suffering, dear brothers and sisters, because you have remained strong in your faith.*

—1 Thessalonians 3:7

WE CAN ALL USE ENCOURAGEMENT IN LIVING THE Christian life. The *Holy Bible* is full of stories that give us hope, joy, and inspiration. They are timeless stories of people facing challenges that we can each relate to throughout the many ups and downs, the triumphs and tragedies we face in this journey we call our earthly life.

At those times when you become beaten down and discouraged, I pray that you are able to recall these and other stories of faith, hope, and courage from Scripture to strengthen and motivate you to stay the course and go the distance in your relationship with Jesus Christ. As Galatians 6:9 exhorts us, "So let's not get tired of doing what is good. At just the right time we will reap a harvest of blessing if we don't give up."

# David

*David replied to the Philistine, "You come to me with sword, spear, and javelin, but I come to you in the name of the Lord of Heaven's Armies—the God of the armies of Israel, whom you have defied."*
—1 Samuel 17:45

The story of David in Scripture begins with an overlooked shepherd boy, and ends with the greatest earthly king Israel had ever known.

Scripture tells us that David was "a man after God's own heart" (1 Samuel 13:14, Acts 13:22). He was the whole package—the *real* deal. David had a strength of character, integrity, and a heart that longed to please and obey God. Yet, in spite of all those characteristics, with good looks and musical talent to boot, David was often dismissed and overlooked. Even Samuel, Israel's prophet, priest, and judge failed to recognize David as God's anointed when sent to search him out among Jesse's sons.

Do you ever feel overlooked like David?

He was the youngest of Jesse's seven sons, so in terms of the pecking order, David was the clean-up crew. But, being at the tail end of things has its advantages. David became a skilled warrior, fearless in battle. He slayed lions, bears and anything else that threatened his flock. He slayed the Philistine giant, Goliath, by means of a stone and slingshot. This victory garnered the attention of King Saul, who was quick to bring David into his service. But, as is often the case when our actions are blessed by God, others become jealous. David became a great warrior in battle. When the young women in Israel began to chant that Saul had slayed his thousands and David his ten thousands, King Saul determined in his heart to kill David.

But, God protected David. Time and time and time again, God made a way for David.

The Book of Psalms recounts the many emotions David felt throughout his struggles. Psalm 42:3 says, "Day and night I have only tears *for* food, while my enemies continually taunt me, saying, 'Where is this God of yours?'" Have you ever felt like that?

In spite of David's many struggles, he never failed to praise God, to thank God, and to believe in God's divine plan for his life. Do you praise Him, thank Him, and believe in His divine plan for your life?

David wasn't perfect. He made some pretty big mistakes in his life—just like you and me. But he repented of his sin and turned his life back to God after doing so.

Do you ever feel overlooked or forgotten? Like David, do you feel betrayed by the very people you should be depending on to help you in life? Always remember that God sees you. You haven't been overlooked. He knows just what you're going through, right this very moment, and He has a divine plan for your life.

Where others see a shepherd boy, God may see a king.

# Joseph

*You intended to harm me, but God intended it all for good. He brought me to this position so I could save the lives of many people.*
—*Genesis 50:20*

Though we mentioned Joseph briefly in Chapter Four, his story is worth repeating in greater detail.

Joseph was his father's favorite son. He was the eldest of two children born to Rachel, Jacob's favorite wife. The *Holy Bible* tells us in Genesis 37:3, "Jacob loved Joseph more than any of his other children because Joseph had been born to him in his old age."

This favoritism was no secret in the family. Joseph was sent regularly to check up on his brothers, sons of Leah. And, Jacob even gave Joseph a special robe to show his "much loved" status, perpetuating the jealousy between the brothers.

One day, Joseph told his brothers about a dream he had in which they all bowed down to him. The wedge between the brothers had, by this time, become a chasm.

The next time Jacob sent Joseph to check up on his brothers, they plotted to kill him. But, Reuben, the oldest, came to Joseph's rescue and convinced the brothers not to kill him. They threw Joseph into a well, then sold him as a slave to a band of Ishmaelite traders. The brothers then put animal blood all over Joseph's beautiful robe and concocted a story about him being killed by wild animals to tell their father, Jacob.

But the story of Joseph is only beginning here. He goes on to work as a slave in the house of Potiphar, who was Captain of the Palace Guard for the Egyptian Pharaoh. The Lord was with Joseph, enabling him to succeed at everything he touched. Potiphar could see this and placed Joseph in charge of everything he owned.

Meanwhile, Potiphar's wife wanted some touching of her own and continued to proposition Joseph. Joseph was an honorable man and resisted her every advance, doing his best to stay away from her as much as possible. One day, Potiphar's wife caught Joseph when no one else was around. She grabbed his cloak and demanded that he sleep with her. Joseph ran from the house, but Potiphar's wife was still holding his cloak. She began to scream and told the servants Joseph tried to molest her.

When Potiphar heard his wife's story, he was furious and threw Joseph in jail.

God was with Joseph in jail, too. He became the favorite of the prison warden. Soon, he was in charge of everything in the prison, too, and all that he touched succeeded.

When God gave Joseph the interpretation of Pharaoh's dream in prison, the Pharaoh was so grateful that he made Joseph the second in command of his entire kingdom! Talk about being catapulted to the top! Joseph went from the jailhouse to the king's house in a moment's time!

Do you know that God can do that for you, too?

But, the story doesn't end there. When Joseph's brothers came to

Egypt for food during a time of great famine, God brought a day of reckoning. You can read the entire story in Genesis 39-45. Joseph recognized them, but they didn't recognize him. After playing with them for a bit, Joseph revealed his true identity. The brothers' sin brought great fear, but Joseph offered great love and forgiveness to them, knowing that God used their evil intent for good in his life.

Never forget Romans 8:28, "And we know that God causes everything to work together for the good of those who love God and are called according to his purpose for them."

God can use the evil intent of others for good in your life, too.

## Daniel

*Then he said, "Don't be afraid, Daniel. Since the first day you began to pray for understanding and to humble yourself before your God, your request has been heard in heaven. I have come in answer to your prayer."—Daniel 10:12*

Daniel was a man who loved God and was determined to keep himself pure and undefiled. Not only that, but the *Holy Bible* tells us he was strong, healthy, good-looking, intelligent, knowledgeable, had good judgment, and had been given the gift of interpreting dreams and visions. He was definitely not your average fella. You can read his story in the Book of Daniel.

He was a mighty prayer warrior, too. Daniel prayed to God, the one true and living God, three times a day with windows open, facing Jerusalem. And, he always gave thanks to God.

Not everyone likes the over-achiever like Daniel. Those whose hearts are bent on sin would rather see the standard lowered to their level than raised to God's.

When Darius the Mede was king, he found Daniel to be more capable than any other leader in his kingdom, so King Darius planned to set Daniel in charge of the entire kingdom. When the other administrators and officers learned this, they devised a scheme to entrap Daniel and stop the king's plan. They convinced King Darius to make a law that anyone who worships someone, divine or human, besides the king should be thrown into the lion's den, and the king agreed.

It wasn't long before they all ran tattling to King Darius that Daniel was breaking the king's law and must be thrown into the den of lions. Reluctantly, the king had Daniel lowered into the den of lions.

The next morning, King Darius couldn't wait to rush out and check to see if God had rescued Daniel. He was overjoyed to hear Daniel shout, "Long live the king!" God had sent an angel to shut the mouths of the lions! The king then had the officers and administrators who schemed against Daniel thrown into the den of lions with their families. The lions tore them to shreds before they even touched the ground.

But, what does that mean to you and to me?

In this life, we face many schemers who would dream of our demise as we try to follow God's way. But, be encouraged. The same God that sent an angel to close the mouths of the lions for Daniel can close the mouths of the lions you face today, too.

## Shadrach, Meshach and Abednego

Shadrach, Meshach, and Abednego replied, "O Nebuchadnezzar, we do not need to defend ourselves before you. If we are thrown into the blazing furnace, the God whom we serve is able to save us. He will rescue us from your power, Your Majesty. But even if he doesn't, we want to make it clear to you, Your Majesty, that we will never serve your gods or worship the gold statue you have set up." –Daniel 3:6-18

I love the pure, simple confidence and faith of Shadrach, Meshach and Abednego in this verse of Scripture. They don't speak arrogantly to the king. They merely state what they know to be true as God's children. The simplicity of their words, God's truth, is powerful.

We don't know an awful lot about Shadrach, Meshach and Abednego. We know that they were from royal or noble Judean families taken captive by the Babylonians. They were chosen, along with Daniel, for their elite status, good looks, strength, education, and overall ability to serve in the palace.

Their birth names were Hananiah, Mishael, and Azariah, but they were renamed by King Nebuchadnezzar's chief of staff. By whatever name these men were called, their faith in God never wavered.

When the king made a gold statue that was ninety feet high and nine feet wide, he commanded that all his subjects bow down and worship the statue at the sound of the music or immediately be thrown into the fiery furnace.

Shadrach, Meshach and Abednego refused to compromise their beliefs, and stood firm in their faith. Meanwhile, there were some astrologers who were quick to tattle on the trio, hoping to gain favor with the king.

When King Nebuchadnezzar found out about it, he was angry, but he gave the men one more chance to bow down and worship the statue. When they shared God's truth with the king—showing no fear of the earthly consequence for their obedience to God—King Nebuchadnezzar was so furious that the *Holy Bible* tells us the king's face became distorted with rage. He had the furnace heated seven times hotter than usual, and they were thrown in securely tied and fully clothed. The furnace was so hot that the soldiers who threw Shadrach, Meshach and Abednego into the furnace were killed by the heat.

Read Daniel 3:24-30.

King Nebuchadnezzar's advisers looked into the furnace and saw four men in the furnace, not three, and one looked different than the others. They were all walking around, untied. When Nebuchadnezzar took them out of the furnace, not only had they not been burned, but their clothing wasn't singed, and they did not even smell of smoke! It was enough to make even an unbelieving king believe in the One true and living God.

When we refuse to compromise our faith in God and in Jesus Christ, His Son, we open the door to enable miracles like this to occur. We need only believe, and open our eyes to see them. Look around you. Do you believe?

# Job

*There once was a man named Job who lived in the land of Uz. He was blameless—a man of complete integrity. He feared God and stayed away from evil.—Job 1:1*

Sometimes it's hard to understand why bad things happen to *good* people. Though we know there is none *good* but God (Mark 10:18), we also know that if we obey the commands of God, there is an expectation that things will go well for us and for our family (Deuteronomy 12:28). It was no different in Job's day, for Job.

Job was a man who feared God, and as the verse above tells us, he stayed away from evil, too. And, God had been good to Job; that is, until Satan got permission from God to test Job and his relationship with God.

Job experienced some pretty terrible circumstances at the hands of Satan, including the loss of all of his children, all of his wealth, and his health. You can read the entire story in the Book of Job.

But Job never lost his faith in God, and the end of his life was blessed more than the beginning.

Job had trouble understanding all of the *why* behind what happened to him, but he knew it was not of his own making, and he continued to trust that God had a plan.

Have you ever felt like Job? Are you going through difficult circumstances that aren't of your own making or choosing?

Take heart. We may not always understand why things happen.

But, just as surely as God had a plan for Job, to prosper him and not to harm him, to give him a future and a hope, God has a plan for you, too (Jeremiah 29:11).

## Esther

*"If you keep quiet at a time like this, deliverance and relief for the Jews will arise from some other place, but you and your relatives will die. Who knows if perhaps you were made queen for just such a time as this?"*
—Esther 4:14

Have you ever been surprised to find yourself elevated to a position that was beyond anything you ever dreamed? That is what happened to Esther. She went from pauper to palace in a moment's time, and became queen after just a year of preparation. Let me tell you a small piece of her story.

Esther was an orphaned Jewish girl who had been taken into the family of her older cousin, Mordecai, and raised as his daughter. She was a very beautiful girl.

When King Xerxes became displeased with Queen Vashti after her refusal to come to the palace and allow everyone to gaze on her beauty at his royal banquet, she was forever banished from the king's presence. And so, the search was on for a new queen to take her place. King Xerxes sent agents to scour the land in search of all the beautiful young virgins to be brought to the palace. It was decided that the one who most pleased the king would become queen in Vashti's place.

King Xerxes was most pleased with Esther, and she became queen.

But, Mordecai was still in the picture, watching out for his young cousin, and for the Jewish race. He worked at the king's gate and was a very loyal soul. When Mordecai heard about an assassination attempt against the king, he reported it to Esther and the plot was foiled.

Later, when Haman, the king's highest official, plotted to wipe out the Jewish race by decree of the king, Mordecai reminded Esther that she was in a position, perhaps the position to save her people, the Jews.

Esther was nervous and apprehensive, but she also knew that she had to do what was right. She had to save her people. So, she invited Haman and the king to a banquet in their honor. She was too nervous to tell the king of Haman's plot at this banquet, so she invited them to another banquet the following night. Here, Esther finally had the nerve to tell King Xerxes all that Haman had done, and revealing her true identity as a Jew. She found favor in the eyes of her king, Haman was put to death, and Mordecai moved from the king's gate to wearing the king's signet ring. Most importantly, the Jewish race was saved.

Esther's privilege was a gift to be shared. It was a position of great power, and of immense responsibility. Scripture tells us in the second half of Luke 12:48, "When someone has been given much, much will be required in return; and when someone has been entrusted with much, even more will be required."

Do you find yourself in a position of privilege or power? Have you been entrusted with much? Are you using your power, privilege and/or wealth in obedience to God? Perhaps, like Esther, God has blessed you so that you might use this blessing for just such a time as this.

# Abraham

*And because of Abraham's faith, God counted him as righteous.*
*—Romans 4:22*

Abraham is considered the father of the Jewish race, yet he was seventy-five years old when God first called him to leave his homeland of Haran. You can read about him in Genesis Chapter Twelve through Twenty-three.

Abram, as he was first called, was to go to a place that God would show him, but he had no idea where that place was, or how long it would take to get there. God promised to make Abram into a great nation, to make him famous, to bless him and make him a blessing to others. God promised to curse those who treated him with contempt, and he even told Abram that all nations, all the families on earth, would be blessed through him.

Many people today would think that Abram was imagining things or that surely he misunderstood God. They may have forgotten that His ways are not our ways (Isaiah 55:8-9). Our God is unconventional. He is both wonderful and radical.

This is what makes Abram—later renamed *Abraham*—different. He believed God. He took the promises of God at face value, and he trusted that God would do what He said He would do.

His faith was tested repeatedly, and although he wasn't perfect, Abraham believed God, and he acted in obedience to Him based on that belief.

When Abraham was nearly one hundred years old with no children, he still believed God and trusted that somehow, some way, God would make him a father of many nations. And, when God delivered Isaac, the son of promise, Abraham could see the vision of the promise fulfilled through the eyes of faith.

May you be encouraged today to have that same kind of faith—the kind of faith the *Holy Bible* teaches us to have. This kind of faith and trust in God, His plans, and His purposes can move mountains, heal the sick, raise the dead, cast out demons, and help feed your next door neighbor.

May you be filled with this kind of faith today and always.

## Noah

*This is the account of Noah and his family. Noah was a righteous man, the only blameless person living on earth at the time, and he walked in close fellowship with God.*—Genesis 6:9

You are probably familiar with Noah and the ark, but do you really know Noah's story? I encourage you to read it in Genesis Chapter Six through Chapter Nine, even if you have read it many times before.

Noah's story is one of a man who loved God and longed to please Him. God saw this and rewarded Noah. It is so wonderful and comforting to know that the God of the Universe always sees us. He sees the deepest longing of each and every heart, whether it is set on pleasing Him or not. And, God rewards those who long to please Him, following after Him with single-minded love.

Another piece of the story of Noah that is a tremendous encouragement is his complete obedience. Noah did not cut corners when it came to doing what God commanded. Scripture tells us in Genesis 6:22, "So Noah did everything exactly as God had commanded him."

Do you complete each and every task exactly as God commands?

The *Holy Bible* tells us that Noah was the only righteous person living in his day, and that he walked in close fellowship with God. In light of that information, we can assume there was no shortage of criticism and ridicule as Noah went about completing each and every task exactly as God had commanded him. It would be hard to have any type of fellowship with the evil people surrounding him.

But, God saw it all, and Noah found grace, he found favor in the eyes of God. To walk in close fellowship with the Father is to be valued above anything and everything the world could ever offer us.

Are you facing pressure from evil people? Are they tempting you and enticing you with all that the world has to offer?

My friend, remember Noah. And, remember that nothing the world has to offer us could ever compare to a close personal relationship with God.

Do you know how desperately He loves you and how closely He watches you?

If God delivered Noah and his family from the flood that destroyed the world, He can deliver you from whatever you're facing today.

## Moses

*Now Moses was very humble—more humble than any other person on earth.—Numbers 12:3*

Humility is a quality that is important to God. The *Holy Bible* tells us in James 4:10, "Humble yourselves before the Lord, and he will lift you up in honor." And, that is exactly what He did for Moses.

Moses' story is miraculous from beginning to end. As a baby he was rescued out of the Nile River from certain death at Pharaoh's decree by the Pharaoh's own daughter. Pharaoh's daughter unknowingly hired his own mother to care for him. God had His hand upon Moses throughout his life.

When Moses came upon God in the burning bush, God called him to lead His people, Israel, out of their oppression in Egypt. In his humility, Moses would have never envisioned himself in such a position. In fact, he argued and even pleaded with God that he was not qualified or worthy of the position. But, God promised to be with Moses, and to send his brother, Aaron, to assist him.

And, God *was* with Moses.

When Pharaoh refused to let the Israelites leave Egypt, God sent ten plagues until finally let them go. God even parted the Red Sea so that His people could walk across on dry land and escape slavery in Egypt. You can read the entire account beginning in Exodus Chapter Two.

By the mighty hand of God, a humble servant was able to be His instrument to deliver an entire nation of people from slavery into the Promised Land.

Just imagine what He can do through you.

# Abigail

*This man's name was Nabal, and his wife, Abigail, was a sensible and beautiful woman. But Nabal, a descendant of Caleb, was crude and mean in all his dealings.*—1 Samuel 25:3

The story of Abigail and her evil husband, Nabal, would be incomplete without the mention of the anointed king of Israel, David.

As our story begins, David and his band of ruddy followers have camped among Nabal's shepherds providing a wall of protection for them during sheep shearing time. It was a time of celebration. So, David sent ten of his men to ask Nabal if he would be willing to share any provisions they had in exchange for the kindness and protection they provided Nabal's men during this important time.

True to his nature, Nabal responded cruelly and foolishly to David's men, refusing them any kindness. When David received word of Nabal's response, he told his men to get their swords.

Meanwhile, Nabal's shepherds, hearing the exchange between their master and David's men, quickly ran to tell Abigail in hopes she could do something, anything to help them avoid an almost certain demise. Abigail immediately loaded bread, wine, sheep, grain, raisins, and fig cakes on donkeys and had her servants send them ahead of her to David and his men. Abigail followed shortly thereafter, but she did not tell her husband, Nabal, what she was doing.

As Abigail neared David, she got off the donkey and bowed before David, taking full responsibility for the foolish behavior of her husband, and letting David know that she knew nothing of the men he had sent. David praised God for Abigail's wisdom and good judgment, promising not to harm Nabal or anyone in her household.

When Abigail returned home, her husband was drunk, celebrating with a big party. The next morning when Nabal was sober, Abigail told him all that had happened with David. This caused Nabal to have a stroke, and he lay paralyzed until God struck him dead ten days later. When David learned what happened to Nabal, he sent his men to ask Abigail to be his wife.

Maybe you feel like Abigail. You may be married to or partnered with a cruel and foolish person like Nabal. Remember that God sees your heart, and He sees theirs, too.

Isaiah 54:5 tells us, "For your Creator will be your husband; the Lord of Heaven's Armies is his name! He is your Redeemer, the Holy One of Israel, the God of all the earth."

## Hannah

*Then Hannah prayed: "My heart rejoices in the Lord! The Lord has made me strong. Now I have an answer for my enemies; I rejoice because you rescued me.—1 Samuel 2:1*

God's timing is not the same as our timing. His omniscience and omnipotence allow Him access and understanding that we do not have. And, He always uses it for the good of those who love Him and are called according to His purposes—always.

Hannah is a wonderful example of this. Her story begins in First Samuel Chapter One.

Hannah was one of two women married to Elkanah. She had no children, but Elkanah's other wife, Peninnah had children. Each year when they went to the Tabernacle for Elkanah to present his sacrifices to the Lord, he would give portions of the meat to Peninnah and each of her children, but he would give only one portion to Hannah because God had given her no children. It probably wouldn't have been so bad for Hannah had it not been for Peninnah taunting her for not being able to have children. Each year Peninnah would taunt Hannah, and each year Hannah was reduced to tears, not even able to eat.

Elkanah loved Hannah, and Scripture tells us he tried to comfort her, as 1 Samuel 1:8 tells us, "Why are you crying, Hannah?" Elkanah would ask. "Why aren't you eating? Why be downhearted just because you have no children? You have me—isn't that better than having ten sons?"

But, Hannah was downhearted; so much so that she got up from the meal to pray, and crying bitterly she made a vow that if God would give her a son, she would give him back to God. As a sign of the vow, his hair would never be cut. As the priest, Eli, watched Hannah, he thought she was drunk because he saw her lips moving and heard no sound. When he realized she was simply praying in earnest, he sent her away in peace, and affirmed that God may answer her request.

And, God did.

God blessed Hannah with a son, Samuel. And, Hannah honored her vow by giving her son back to God. And, God blessed Hannah with three more sons and two daughters to fill her life and bring comfort to her.

Have you ever cried bitterly to God? Distraught and downhearted, have you brought your request before Him? He hears your prayer, and His ways and timing are perfect (2 Samuel 22:31).

When God answered Hannah's request, she offered a prayer of praise. The *Holy Bible* tells us in First Samuel 2:1, "Then Hannah prayed: 'My heart rejoices in the Lord! The Lord has made me strong. Now I have an answer for my enemies; I rejoice because you rescued me.'"

Do you need an answer for your enemies? The Lord can rescue you, too.

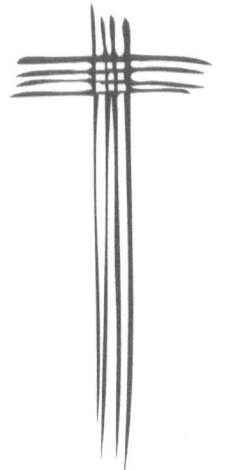

# *eight*

## The Journey

I started on a journey that I didn't plan to take
While minding my own business on a road down by the lake

A man there saw me fishin'—I was struggling with my line
His face was kind and gentle, and his eyes saw clear through mine

He said, "I'd like to help you—I can show you a new way"
My friends, they all ignored him—my heart longed for him to stay

"Sir," I said, "Please tell me . . . what is this new way you know
I only know this one way—show me, please, before you go"

The man, he took my fishing line and cast it on the lake
His hands were sure and confident, the cast made not a wake

# Discipled

*There was no hesitation as he reeled the line back in*
*The fish he caught was massive, I could see from just the fin*

*"Tell me, sir, your secret, if you please, before you go*
*What makes your way so different—tell me, please, I've got to know"*

*"The Father is the difference—He sent His Son from up above*
*To show the world His mercy, to give each one His love"*

*"How can I have this difference, sir, can it come down to me*
*I want the peace I see in you, I want this love I see"*

*"Receive His one and only Son, that's how to have real life*
*Repent of sin, believe in Him, abandon this world's strife"*

*I did what this man told me and was baptized at the lake*
*My life is filled with joy, for now a different path I take.*

# About the Author

PRISCILLA DOREMUS BECAME A CHRISTIAN AT THE AGE OF five years, and longs to serve God in every area of her life. She has a passion for sharing His love with others. Priscilla is the daughter of a minister, a graduate of Baylor University, and mother of two. She teaches a discipleship class to the youth in her local church. Priscilla and her family currently make their home in Sugar Land, Texas. She is also the author of *Prayers for Times of Crisis*, *Focus: A Daily Devotional*, *Focused Daily on God's Best*, and *Plea Bargain*. For more information, please see the author's blog: www.priscilladoremus.com.

# Helpful Resources

IN ADDITION TO THE *HOLY BIBLE*, FOLLOWING ARE BUT A few resources the author has found helpful and encouraging in living the Christian life:

## Books

*Pilgrim's Progress* by John Bunyan
*The Screwtape Letters* by C. S. Lewis
*The Basket of Flowers* by Christoph von Schmid
*That Printer of Udell's* by Harold Bell Wright
*My Utmost for His Highest* by Oswald Chambers
*Storm Warning* by Billy Graham
*Heaven is For Real* by Todd Burpo
*The Love Dare* by Stephen and Alex Kendrick
*Return from Tomorrow* by George G. Ritchie with Elizabeth Sherrill
*The Boy Who Went to Heaven* by Kevin and Alex Malarkey

## Movies

*Pilgrim's Progress*
*God's Not Dead*
*God's Not Dead 2*

*I'm Not Ashamed*
*Soul Surfer*
*Miracles from Heaven*
*The Hiding Place*
*Courageous*
*Fireproof*
*Facing the Giants*
*Fly Wheel*
*The Case for Christ*
*War Room*
*Heaven is for Real*

## Musical Artists

Aaron Jeoffrey
Bradley Walker
Casting Crowns
Dallas Holm
David Meece
DeGarmo & Key
Evie
Francesca Battistelli
The Imperials
Kathy Troccoli
Keith Green
Larnelle Harris

MercyMe

Michael W. Smith

Point of Grace

Russ Taff

Selah

Shane Harper

Steve Camp

Steven Curtis Chapman

TobyMac

Twila Paris

Wayne Watson

# Websites

www.biblegateway.com

www.lamplighter.net

www.crosswalk.com

www.intouch.org

www.lwf.org

www.billygraham.org

www.odb.org

www.utmost.org

www.ingramcontent.com/pod-product-compliance
Lightning Source LLC
Chambersburg PA
CBHW021118080526
44587CB00010B/557